# YORUBA BEADWORK

# YORUBA BEADWORK

## ART OF NIGERIA

By WILLIAM FAGG

Edited and with a Foreword by Bryce Holcombe

Descriptive Catalogue by John Pemberton

*Cover:*
*A beaded dance panel,* yata.
*13¾" × 12½"*
*See Plate 6.*

Published in the United States of America in 1980 by
Rizzoli International Publications, Inc.
712 Fifth Avenue, New York, N.Y. 10019
in cooperation with The Pace Gallery, New York

LC 80-51621
ISBN 0-8478-0347-3

# CONTENTS

*Fig. 1: The old crown of the Ogoga of Ikere, 31". Paul and Ruth Tishman Collection.*

# FOREWORD

The inspiration for an exhibition of Yoruba beadwork came from two remarkable beaded crowns, one in the collection of Paul Tishman and one that I was able to acquire for the collection of Dr. Milton Ratner. These magnificent objects of great sculptural and graphic quality inspired me to examine the entire range of Yoruba beadwork and to assemble over a period of several years an extraordinary collection of traditional beaded objects — the crowns, staffs, and scepters which comprise the regalia of kings and the divination bags and dance panels of the priests and devotees of important sacred cults.

In the case of African beadwork, ethnographic information is not equal to our aesthetic appreciation. As a result, we are seldom able to individually identify the creative hands that have fashioned these beautiful works of art. We hope this exhibition and this volume will help to establish the importance of these objects in the history of African Art. We salute the unique achievement of these talented people, who will, for the most part, forever remain anonymous.

I would like to extend my personal gratitude to Mr. William Fagg for his interest and for his text. He was for many years the Deputy Keeper of the African Collections of the British Museum. As the outstanding authority on all phases of Nigerian art and particularly that of the Yoruba, it is a privilege to have him associated with this project. We are indebted to Mr. John Pemberton, Crosby Professor of Religion at Amherst College, for his identification of the iconography and symbolism of these objects, which is a major scholarly contribution. For the past ten years he has studied ritual symbolism and cult organization in Northern Yorubaland, and his insights are particularly valuable. The exhibition would not have been possible without the patience and skill of Ms. Francesca Fleming. For continuous support, I want to thank Lisa Bradley and my colleagues at The Pace Gallery.

Bryce Holcombe
Director, Primitive Art
The Pace Gallery

Fig. 2: The Deji of Akure,
Ademuwagun Adesida II,
wearing ceremonial beaded
dress.

# *Beaded decorations,*

made of various kinds of perishable materials, were probably part of the equipment of the genus *Homo* very soon after he became *sapiens* in the Middle to Late Paleolithic; so much may we deduce from early evidences of the development of art in man. Long before their appearance in the archaeological record, beads in the form of "found objects" or simple wood or clay artifacts must have followed the tying of the first knot in a thong or a piece of string.

We shall not attempt to trace the development of beads and beadwork in the world or even in Africa. They are almost ubiquitous in the proto-historic and historic periods in all continents. Unfortunately, beads are notoriously difficult to use in studies of the diffusion of culture traits because of the extreme ease with which they can be used in trade and their inherent reproducibility, which often means that physicists must be called in to unmask their origins.

We are concerned here with a single manifestation of beadwork among the Yoruba of Western Nigeria and Dahomey (Benin) in the nineteenth and twentieth centuries, a wondrous flowering of their traditional art which is based on the sudden availability from Europe of "seed beads," tiny trade beads in an almost limitless palette of colors, and regular in size (about two millimeters). Their small size and great variety of colors seem to have inspired the Yoruba to produce what was in effect a whole new art form which owed nothing except the basic beads to outside sources. (Beads of comparable size and color have been available for centuries from Arab and Persian sources in the islands and the mainland littoral of East Africa, from the Horn to Sofala in Mozambique. However, they do not seem to have penetrated to West Africa as the Indian Ocean cowrie shells did on a great scale.)

## The cult of kings

Among the Yoruba, as among many tribal peoples of the world who have stratified societies with a sacral kingship of long standing, the means of adornment in dress tend to cluster about the ruler and his court — whereas "acephalous" or unstratified societies often favor decoration of the body by scarification for all men, regardless of class or rank. From the earliest times — the apogee of ancient Ife — Yoruba monarchy, though by no means absolute, seems to have exerted at least as much power, and also sanctity, as it did during the nineteenth century. (We must remember that in this century the kings lost perhaps nine-tenths of their power to colonial governments and later to the state, and that as with other aspects of tribal life in its terminal phases, the evidential value of modern phenomena is therefore considerably impaired.)

At Ife, nearly a thousand years ago, the Onis or priest-kings are shown in the surviving bronzes and terracottas to have worn a very great weight of beads that were each up to about a half-inch in length. We know something of their color, since some of the strands of beads are painted red. We do not know the state in which the bronzes were meant to be seen. It is not known whether the unpainted strands represented green beads as they now appear, or were painted other colors which have not survived. It is also difficult to say whether any beadwork, in our sense of beaded embroidery, is present in the corpus, as opposed to massed necklaces in tidy order, but it is certainly possible. In the case of some of the bronze heads, rows of holes outlining the moustache and beard held small black glass beads not very much larger than "seed" beads, but less regular in size, at the time they were buried, which may not be more than a century ago. They were arranged in the form of a beaded curtain covering the lower part of the face. The original purpose of the holes is, however, still uncertain.

There was a great bead-making industry at Ife during the classical period (about 1000-1500 A.D.) which produced beads of several beautiful shades. Frank Willett now considers this industry to have been a secondary one, which melted down beads obtained from elsewhere, apparently both from Medieval Europe and the Islamic world. It certainly appears that some secondary work was carried on (as indeed might be expected even in a primary industry, especially in West Africa, where there was a tendency to use materials more than once); but the probability, based on the work of physicists, that the industry was wholly secondary, does not yet appear to be established. In any case, this great industry languished and was forgotten, presumably after the classical period. At Igbo Idio, for example, the most sacred and ancient of the innumerable shrines of Ile-Ife, where the three founding gods — including Odudua — first brought up earth from the sea, the most revered relic is "Odudua's drum," a large and now fragmentary bead-making crucible.

We have little information on the nature of the crowns and other regalia worn by the Yoruba Obas in the sixteenth to eighteenth centuries. But the strings of red-painted beads on the Oni's robes in the classical period may provide a hint of continuity, if, as is likely, the beads were of cornelian or other red stone of the types now often known as "Ilorin beads" in Nigeria, although, in fact, they came from farther west, passing through and often being processed in Ilorin. Certainly they have continued to reach Benin (whose kingship was under Ife influence) from at least 1550 to the present, and they have played an essential part in the regalia, along with the smaller beads of red coral whose origin is in the Balearic Islands.

Here, perhaps, *ade Odudua,* Odudua's crown, may be of interest (Fig. 6). Of course, we need not attribute to it anything like the antiquity which its name implies, but it appears to date at least from the eighteenth century, before the seed-bead crowns were thought of. It is the property of the Owa of Idanre, and on April 4, 1959, I clambered up the precipitous cliff face by

Fig. 3: The Araba, Chief Ifa
Priest at Lagos, in procession
during the annual festival.

a steep stairway to the old fortress village to interview the Owa, who was very shortly afterward to abandon the old town to rule his people in New Idanre below. The crown was brought out for me in the palace. It has an amorphous and untidy appearance, but consists largely of strings of red beads which are mostly stone but may include some coral (the town is separated only by the dense Idanre forest from the Benin kingdom, from which the coral would have come). It also includes a rather miscellaneous assortment of other beads. The Owa had been told that the crown had been added to, before his time, but he did not know which strands were the added ones. He agreed that it originally seemed to have been a red "coral" crown. It is not very much like the Benin coral-and-cornelian crowns, but does look like the ancestor of the falling curtains of seed beads on the crowns of the nineteenth and twentieth centuries.

The right to wear crowns is in the gift of the Oni of Ife, by common consent, since all Yoruba kings are reputed descendants of sons of Odudua (who is, however, worshipped as a goddess over important areas of south and west Yorubaland). There are always said to be only sixteen "crowned Obas," but this is merely an accepted fiction, and no two lists agree (although nearly all agree on the Oba of Benin as the only ruler of a non-Yoruba people). I should guess that the number of crown-wearing Obas may in fact be as many as fifty or more, and some of the finest and most elaborate collections are in the possession of very minor rulers. The magnificient crown worn by the ruler of Odogbolu, a little village near Ijebu-Ode, which adorned the cover of *African Arts,* Vol. III, No. 3, 1970, is a case in point (and the accompanying article, "The Sign of the Divine King," by Professor R.F. Thompson, is a rich source of information and hypotheses on the subject).

The most spectacular array of beaded regalia that I have seen was also at a village on the outskirts of Ijebu-Ode in 1950, when the Dagburewe of Idowa had them displayed for me as a demonstration of the antiquity of his throne (Fig. 9). The crowns were said to be very old and the wood staffs to have been added at the rate of one for each Dagburewe. But I thought it unlikely that any of the crowns could be earlier than about 1900, and the staffs all seemed to be of much the same age.

I have suggested elsewhere (*The Living Arts of Nigeria,* 1970) that, because of their strategic position close to Ife, the invention of the new style of crown was probably due to the Adeshina family of Efon-Alaye, who, besides being one of the greatest Yoruba carving families, make crowns for most of the Obas over a great part of the country. Though they usually go to live as guests of an Oba while making a crown for him, some of the family appear to have settled at centers far from their homes, and this perhaps accounts for the uniformity of style throughout Yorubaland. Olowe of Ise, the great carver, is said to have migrated from Efon early in his life. There is an intriguing possibility, if he was an Adeshina and a crown-maker before

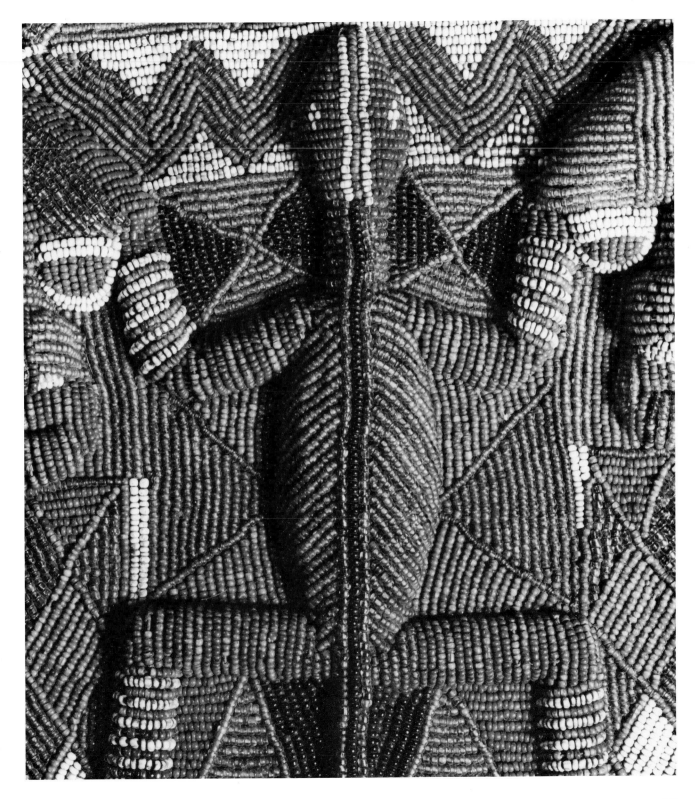

becoming famous as a carver, which might now be hard to verify, that we could attribute to his hand the crown from Ikere, now owned by Paul Tishman (Fig. 1). Two such decisive innovations in the freeing of the human figure from the background as are found both in this crown and the carving of such palace doors as those of Ikere, now in the collection of the Museum of Mankind, would be altogether too much of a coincidence.

## The Ifa cult

This ancient system of divination provides the fundamental coordinates of the Yoruba world — the number four and its multiples. Most of the infinitely variable myths of creation in the Yoruba cosmogony give a place to Orunmila, the *orisha* or god who personifies Ifa, along with Obatala and Odudua, in the original mission entrusted to them by Olorun or Olodumare, the supreme god, to found the world at Ife, the umbilicus like the ancient Greek divination center at Delphi.

The work of Ifa is done by the diviner or *babalawo* ("father of the mystery") with a well-defined set of instruments: the *opele,* two strands of eight split seedpods each, which are thrown and their positions noted in the simpler forms of Ifa; the *agere ifa,* the bowl which holds the sixteen palm nuts which the priest throws from hand to hand to find the right number among the 256 *odu* or cabalistic verses; the *opon* or *pako ifa,* the generally circular wooden tray on which marks are made in wood dust; the *iroke* or

*iro ifa,* or ivory rattle which is also used to spread the wood dust on the tray; the *obuntun* or *ikin ifa,* or small ivory head of Eshu, the activator, which is often placed beside the tray during divination; the large wooden bowl, also called *opon ifa,* which is the general receptacle for the supply of palm nuts and other miscellaneous paraphernalia; and the *orere* or iron rod topped by a bird, which is the diviner's staff of office, stuck in the ground during divination. Of these only the *opele* are sometimes adorned with beads — four strands connecting each of the pods to the next.

It is in the articles of ceremonial or ritual dress, as distinct from the tools of divination, that the important priests of Ifa, and especially the *oluawo,* "lords of the mystery" and the *araba,* who is the supreme head of Ifa

*Fig. 6: Purported crown of Odudua, founder of the Yoruba and one of the three creator gods.*

for each large area of Yorubaland (the Araba of Ife being recognized as *primus inter pares*), shine most splendidly in beaded finery which often rivals that of the Oba himself. The chief articles are a beaded cap, very similar to the "undress" crowns worn nowadays on less important occasions by Obas and scarcely to be distinguished from them; two beaded pouches, suspended from the shoulders by long baldrics; a beaded flywhisk, just like an Oba's; and, often, a beaded walking staff, similarly like an Oba's. Since none of these appears to play any part in the work of divination, it would seem that the explanation must lie in a kind of metaphor of kingship — Ifa being regarded as "king" of all Yoruba cults because it is the most fundamental and most senior.

## The ibeji *or twin cult*

The Yoruba have an unusually high rate of twin births, which they welcome with a guarded optimism, knowing the dangers, physical and spiritual, and the heavy ritual obligations that face them. Upon the death of twins (or a twin) which occurs frequently in these tropical conditions, small wooden surrogates must be carved. They must be washed, fed, clothed and generally tended to as though they were the living twins, and for as long a period as divination may prescribe. It is the most universal and "democratic" of Yoruba cults and does not in itself have anything to do with the royal cult. Yet royal families are not immune to the incidence of twins, and when they are born to a woman of the royal lineage, they may qualify in the event of their death for special beaded garments, doubtlessly ordered from the crown-maker, which may either be individual dresses or double ones, incorporating both the *ere ibeji* in a single wide garment with two neck holes. Similar garments covered with cowrie shells symbolize the dedication of wealth to the cult of the twins and are an alternative to the attachment of strings of cowries to the wrists (which is the reason why all *ibeji* are carved with hands attached to the thighs or occasionally with enlarged hands to retain the strings. Such cowrie-adorned dresses do not imply royal status).

## The cult of Orisha-Oko

This is another cult which has no connection with royalty as such, but in which members who are also members of royal lineages may have specially regal accoutrements made for their cult objects. Orisha Oko is generally said to be the "god of agriculture," but this is inexact. I visited the remote village of Irawo, center of the cult, on March 28, 1959, and interviewed the Ajonrimwin (or king) together with the high priestess of the cult.

They told me that the cult was especially for women who suffered from chronic headaches, presumably migraine, or stomachaches, and were advised by the oracle to go to Irawo to be cured. The principal cult object is the large iron staff, something like a medieval European two-handed broad-

16

sword, called *Opa orisha Oko*. This staff is made to order by Irawo iron-smiths from a sufficient quantity of worn-out hoes which the neophyte is enjoined to bring with her from home. There are thirty of these staffs in the head shrine at Irawo which were apparently the gifts of Obas. I was, however, unable to see these during my short visit, and I do not know whether they were equipped with covers which, I was told, were called *ewu orisha,* dress for the *orisha.* It was impressed upon me that the deity was "too important" to be represented by an image. I asked whether there was any connection with the smallpox god, Shopono; they said "no," though Orisha-Oko will keep smallpox at bay and cure it. I inquired whether he "brings children" and the king replied that he does, "like all the *orisha"* — a pregnant saying, recognizing that most Yoruba are devoted to a single *orisha,* who must therefore provide a "service," to meet all needs of his devotees. The annual festivals of the cult in Irawo are two: *Alano* about September and *Erindun* two months later. At these times the *opa* are brought out from the shrine and leaned against the wall. Part of the new yams must be sacrificed to Orisha-Oko before they can be eaten. Goats, fowl and kola nuts are the other sacrifices made to him. The Ajonrimwin assured me that there were no other cults or carvings in Irawo.

To explain how the *orisha* came by the name, "farm-spirit," they explained that a Moslem priest named Sulemanu (a Moslem form of Solomon) was the first to use the iron staff, having found it standing in the ground on a farm. So the deity is associated with the farm but is not the deity of the farm. Clearly, since the work of women is farming, there will be many con-

*Fig. 9: Regalia of the Dagburewe of Idowa.*

Fig. 10: (overleaf) The Alafin of Oyo with a son and some of his wives.

Fig. 11: Epa mask from Northern Ekiti depicting a female devotee wearing beaded dance panels. Wood, 54". Private Collection.

vergences between deity and farm, for example the collecting of worn-out hoes and the offering of the first new yams (elsewhere associated with various other, not specifically agricultural, cults). Certainly this is one of the more mysterious of Yoruba cults and would repay a thorough anthropological study, based on Irawo. (Only after my visit did it occur to me that I might have asked whether the Orisha Oko is male, as is generally supposed, or female, as I am inclined to think, or both, or neither.)

When I was last on field work, in 1958-59, I did not know of the existence of the beaded *ewu* or dress, knowing only of a version covered with cowrie shells symbolizing wealth, not royalty, of which I collected an example for the British Museum. This would be because the shrines with beaded dresses would have been in the women's quarters of royal palaces, and in those days it was still somewhat *infra dignitatem* for a king to accept money for parting with his cult object. Since then, a rich variety of them, some with small beaded boxes attached to contain pieces of yam, have appeared.

## Other cults

Among the other Yoruba cults in which beadwork is occasionally found is that of the great god of thunder, Shango. A constant feature of his shrines is a series of large square decorated satchels, *laba shango,* the great majority of which are of the same pattern, because they all have to be obtained at great trouble and expense from the Magba, or high priest of the cult, at Oyo. Occasionally, however, a beaded one is found, and these do not conform to a single pattern and are probably of local origin. They may be gifts to a shrine from the Oba of a town, or the link with royalty may be that one of the "avatars" of Shango is said to have been an early Alafin of Oyo.

Both the *Egungun* and the *Gelede* masquerade cults use elaborate dance dresses in bright colors, which may sometimes be embellished with panels of beadwork, such as some examples (probably for *Egungun*) in this exhibition (e.g. Plate 20). We have not exhausted the use of beadwork in the tribal context. Yoruba contemporary painters have gone beyond that context by experimenting with "painting" in seed beads.

## Parallels and contrasts from elsewhere

It is instructive to note how different from the Yoruba case was the situation when the same beads, no doubt from the same sources, were introduced into North America at about the same time, probably early in the nineteenth century. Whereas Yoruba culture was still in full vigor, and would remain autonomous for another century or more in most places, the North American Indian cultures were by then in an advanced stage of "colonization" and "other-orientation" — long before they had been subjected to any real study — and had incorporated many elements of baroque, rococo, and other kinds of feedback. So, when beaded embroidery arrived, it was from the beginning dominated by plant forms and other designs of

European derivation, only slightly differentiated by tribal predilections. From about the same time, collectors began to seek eagerly for Indian objects, under the influence of the infant science of anthropology, but already there was little left on which to found a discipline of study and collection except hybrid objects exhibiting some degree of "feedback," although these, led by the war bonnets, underwent a considerable revival (and assimilation) in the solidarity brought on by the Indian Wars of the mid-nineteenth century.

Let us now look briefly, by way of further contrast, at the only tribal group in West Africa which rivals the Yoruba in their addiction to bead embroidery, the grasslands tribes of Cameroon. In spite of varying origins, these tribes practice a relatively homogeneous style of art, comparable in broad terms to that of the Yoruba. Local variations do indeed exist among the Cameroon grassland tribes, yet hardly more than between the Egba, Oyo, Ekiti and Ijebu in Yorubaland, while in both cases, there is an "over-style" which is immediately discernible. (My assumption is that by 1900, from the point of view of art, the grassland cultures had become assimilated to the point where they could almost be regarded as one tribe.)

In the nineteenth-century Cameroon grasslands a somewhat larger size of trade bead was preferred to the seed beads favored by the Yoruba. (Indeed, the presence of seed beads on grassland figures is generally a sign of a modern forgery, especially if they are set in a nameless black mastic.) Beadwork is employed in two principal ways in the grasslands, both of them differing considerably from Yoruba usage. The first is in the embellishment of dance costumes including cloth masks, well studied by Tamara Northern in her exhibition and catalog, *The Sign of the Leopard,* 1975. The second is in the all-over decoration of wood sculpture, which no other African tribal group attempts to emulate. In the former, what seems at first sight a static and unimaginative system of embroidered straight lines or circles and other simple figures is transformed in the dance into one of the most exciting forms of African dynamism, as the long cloth panels of the "elephant" masks are whirled about and the apparently monotonous rows of beads dissolve into a kaleidoscopic series of broken images. In the second main use of beadwork, however, the dominant consideration seems to have been the correlation: beads = wealth. Beads were added to sculpture not as a means of enhancing its sculptural qualities, but for the purposes of prestige, and with the object of drawing attention to themselves, even, one must suppose, at the expense of the sculpture. The beaded patterns are bold, but they are almost always at variance with the formal structure, showing that the embroiderer and the carver were not in any kind of rapport. I know of only one real exception to this: the magnificent throne in the treasury of Banjum (Bandjoun). The incomparable dynamic rhythms of the two linked figures are dramatically heightened and, as it were, sublimated by the embroiderer's complementary zigzags — demanding, I thought, to be accom-

Fig. 12: *Priestesses of Orisha Oko flanking the emblem of their deity, at Ila-Orangun.*

panied by the brilliant jazzlike passage near the end of Béla Bartók's *Music for Strings, Percussion and Celesta*. This throne, lent by the Fon of Banjum to the Dakar and Paris exhibitions in 1966, is identifiable, though with little impression of its verve, in R. Lecoq, *Les Bamiléké*, 1953, plate 69.

The lack of discipline which generally characterized bead embroidery on three-dimensional sculpture was in its effects not unlike the introduction of European commercial paints to the Yoruba in the latter part of last century. As soon as the emphasis was put on bold and unsubtle color, interest in sculptural form began to wane, and, in one or two generations, it was all but extinct in the Yoruba artistic tradition (for example, *Egungun* masks at Abeokuta, *Gelede* masks in the Lagos area). Grasslands art provides an outstanding example of this phenomenon in the royal statues of Laikom, capital village of the Kom kingdom. Four magnificent figures of Fons (kings) and queens (or queen mothers) made probably in 1855 and 1865, appear to have been covered in beadwork at about the time when the fashion for beadwork coverings was in the course of adoption; one pair now in the Berlin Museum seems to have been carved with beadwork attachments in mind; the other in the Frankfurt Museum and the Katherine White collection, probably not. When these figures were collected by the Germans (1904-5), the replacements then carved, to which the highly prized bead coverings were undoubtedly transferred, including the notorious "Afo-a-Kom," were almost completely devoid of sculptural merit.

The Yoruba, on the other hand, never embarked upon this particular path toward the demise of tribal sculpture. They did occasionally achieve real sculpture in beadwork unsupported by wood, the finest example known being the Tishman crown (Fig. 1) which I photographed at Ikere in 1959. I was told that it was worn by the Ogoga in a dance at the annual New Yams Ceremony, and that it was made for Ogoga Agabaola who reigned from about 1870 to 1880. (This information, from the Ogoga's senior wife, I am inclined to discount, since the piece appears to show awareness of certain sculptural innovations made by the great carver Olowe of Ise in wood sculpture for the Ogoga about 1915).

The above interpretation of the Cameroon data is based on inferences from published material (including that published by Tamara Northern in *Royal Art of Cameroon*, 1973, and in *African Arts*, Vol. IX, No. 3, 1976, pp. 87, 88) which I have not seen published elsewhere, but which seem to me inescapable. Of these inferences, the most important is that the only way in which Germans in 1904-5 could have got away with all four of the Laikom royal sculptures without causing an incident which would still be reverberating around the grasslands to this day was if they had persuaded the Fon to have new figures carved to replace the old ones. This would have been especially so if the Germans agreed to the removal of all the beads to be affixed to the new sculptures, thus completely concealing the substitution, which would in any case be sanctioned by the proper sacrificial rituals.

*Fig. 14: An Ifa divination priest (babalawo) at Ijebu-Igbo with various pieces of his divining equipment.*

The acceptability of this solution would, of course, be all the greater if, as Gebauer reported, the Fon was himself one of the carvers concerned.

There is a very useful self-sealing device in African folk memory, familiar to anyone who has done ethno-historical research in West Africa, whereby if a ritual sculpture has through *force majeure* such as time, or white ant damage, or more latterly by sale, had to be replaced, the event, subject to proper sacrifices, will be entirely forgotten and the age of the original will continue to be attributed to the replacement. This phenomenon can be seen to have muddied the waters at Laikom, as elsewhere in Cameroon. But among the Yoruba, too, it is found to be widely prevalent, and the ethnographer who wishes to be regarded as having his wits about him had better be forewarned of the pitfalls that lie before him in the folkloric quagmire, if he places too great evidential value in the unsupported spoken word.

With material culture, however, our field ethnographer is on firmer ground (although he needs any help that he can get from folklore, social anthropology, and indeed any other discipline at all). Since he is by definition in close contact with the tribal culture, he will not be disturbed by the ceaseless flow of fakes from the urban centers. So he may safely address himself to the properties of matter, from which he may derive, among other things, the stylistic distinctions between individual hands and between tribes, the approximate age of pieces, and the implications of use and wear.

The beadwork of the Yoruba is based on a standardized form of trade beads which are, so to speak, its atoms. Infinite variations are possible within the broad guidelines of Yoruba taste, and indeed, as the color plates suggest, precise repetitions are unknown.

Fig. 15: The Araba's assistant
dancing with beaded bag
and beaded staff at the
annual festival at Lagos.

# PLATES

*Descriptive Catalogue*

*by John Pemberton*

## PLATE 1

A diviner's bag, *apo Ifa,* in which a priest of Ifa carries his divining chain, *opele ifa,* and other objects used in the rites of divination. The priests of Ifa, called *babalawo,* "father of the secret," are highly trained in the skills of divination and in chanting verses from a vast body of oral literature, *Odu Ifa.* Divination proceeds either by manipulation in the diviner's hands of sixteen palm nuts or the toss of an *opele* chain to determine the verses to be recited. The care and seriousness with which the divination rite is performed conveys a world of order, harmony and balance, which contrasts with the troubled spirit of the client. And as the verses of *Odu* are recited, images of others who have suffered similar problems, but who, through divination and sacrifice, discovered configurations of their own lives, are presented to the supplicant. The priests of Ifa are among the few persons permitted to use solidly beaded materials. Such objects are usually reserved for Yoruba kings. A similar bag is in the collection of the Institute of African Studies, University of Ibadan, Nigeria (#670525B).

*10½" × 11¾"*                                                    *Private Collection*

## PLATE 2

A diviner's bag, *apo Ifa*, probably from the Oyo area and used by a diviner whose house worshipped *orisha* Shango. On the shrines for Shango, the deified fourth king of Oyo, whose power is manifest in thunder and lightning, the sculptured wood artifacts are painted red and dotted with white. If the object is of a human figure, the head will be colored with indigo dye. Dance rattles, *shere,* will be covered with a beaded pattern of alternating dark and light colors in a zigzag motif. And prominent on the shrine will be the double-headed dance wands, *oshe Shango,* the motif of which appears in three places in the composition of this Ifa bag.

*11½" × 14"*                                                          *Pace Gallery*

## PLATE 3

A diviner's bag, *apo Ifa,* similar to one illustrated in William Bascom, *Ifa Divination,* Pl. 4a. Bascom attributes the bag to the village of Igana. A diviner is depicted on horseback, carrying his iron staff, *Opa Orere Ifa,* in his right hand. Below is a diviner's tray, *Opon Ifa,* with the face of Eshu at the top. It is Eshu who carries the sacrifices of men to the gods and spirits whose powers effect the course of life in this world. The figure of the *Odu* which appears on the tray is *Ogbe Meji.*

*11" × 11"*                                          *Private collection*

## PLATE 4

Ifa bags, *apo Ifa,* may be double or single. The decorative patterning may be suggested by the Ifa priest or left to the judgement of the beadworker. In the past all
the beadwork was done only upon the commission of an individual object by a
person privileged to use it.

*5¼" × 5¾" each bag*                                              *Pace Gallery*

## PLATE 5

The Orangun of Ila: Ariwajoye I (1967 - Present)
The 24th King, *oba,* of Ila and "Father of the Igbomina Yoruba."

As a direct descendant of one of the sixteen children of Odudua, the god, *orisha,* who aided in the creation of the world and who was the first king of the Yoruba people, the Orangun is one of the few Yoruba kings privileged to wear the veiled beaded crown. Whether it was *orisha* Olokun or *orisha* Obalufon who blessed mankind with the gift of beads, the privilege of their use has traditionally been reserved to kings, to the priests and priestesses of certain gods, and to the herbalist-diviners, that is, to persons whose spiritual powers enable them to move across the boundary that separates man from the gods, the secular from the sacred. It is, however, only to the king that the full range of beaded artifacts is permitted: shoes, fans, flywhisks, footrests, canes, ceremonial staffs, thrones, and crowns.

It is the range of colors and the attribute of luminosity, power to transmit light through matter, to cross boundaries, which make beads an important instrument of religious symbolization.

## PLATE 6

One of a pair of dance panels, *yata*, worn by a devotee of a Yoruba deity, *orisha*, at the time of the annual festival. The faces which appear on many beaded bags and dance panels are visual images of the inner head, *ori inun*, or spiritual power of the worshipper. Thus, as with the prominence of the head in wood sculpture, the image of the face on beaded objects should be understood in terms of the Yoruba concept of *ori*, which means "head," but refers to one's personal destiny. Each person choses his or her *ori* before coming to earth; and although upon being born one forgets what the choice was, the *ori* is like a personal *orisha*, which may be consulted and called upon through divination and sacrifice. While the gods of the Yoruba pantheon may enable one to realize the fullness of one's destiny, they cannot alter it or add to it in any way.

*13¾" × 12½"*                                                    *Pace Gallery*

**PLATE 7**

A diviner's bag, *apo Ifa,* depicting a sailor standing at the edge of the sea. More realistic compositions in which a figure is portrayed against a background are a somewhat recent convention in Yoruba beadwork. Yet reference to the relationship of the individual person to hidden powers, to a deep, mystical, vital energy, maintains a continuity with earlier styles.

*11½" × 13"*                                                              *Private collection*

## PLATE 8

The shining metal staff, *Opa orisha Oko,* the emblem of the deity of the farm, *oko,* is forged from the hoes taken to a blacksmith in Irawo in northwest Yorubaland, who alone may make them. They are "owned" by a male elder of the compound, but the rituals for *orisha* Oko are performed by a priestess, who is a daughter of the house. She is known as the "wife," *iyawo,* of *orisha* Oko. The phallic imagery of the upper portion of the staff is indicated by the priestess's verbal pun on the word *oko,* which may mean farm or penis, depending upon the tonal inflection. The "face" of the deity is in the small square area in the center of the staff. It usually depicts eyes and scarification marks and always has a central cross mark, which is referred to as "the crossroads," *orita.* When sacrifices are made, the devotee will touch her forehead and then the face of the deity with the sacrifice, linking her destiny with his power. She will then place the offering in a whitened calabash in which the foot of the staff rests. The designs on the lower portion of the staff, a large bird and a whirling top, image the power, *ashe,* of *orisha* Oko over witchcraft and the ability of the god and his devotee to move through life with balance and poise.

A. 62½"                                                                  *Pace Gallery*


The staffs of *orisha* Oko are clothed, *ewu,* in beaded sheaths, when they are not the object of ritual attention. Sheaths B and C are characterized by bold, repetitive geometric patterns and sharply contrasting colors, with the depiction of a face at the top. The downward thrust of the series of triangles in B is conveyed in the single image of the lower portion of the shining staff at the center of sheath C. The rich iconographical references in sheath D include a crown with birds, a figure depicting the priestess of *orisha* Oko, another representing the "owner" of the staff, *agbopa,* a royal footrest with a bird perched upon it, as well as the designs that often appear on the staff itself. Although *orisha* Oko was not a deified king, as were some other *orisha,* his importance and power in the life of an agricultural people is such that the emblems of kingship are granted to him.

B. 56"   C. 57"   D. 64"                                                 *Pace Gallery*

47

## PLATE 9

A diviner's bag, *apo Ifa,* the panel of which provides one of the most exciting visual images in the exhibit. Vivid colors are set in contrast. A flash of lightning cuts through, fragmenting, creating tensions within a space set within a larger, more ordered cosmos, providing us with an insight into the Yoruba world of experience.

9½" × 9½"                                                    *Pace Gallery*

## PLATE 10

A beaded and veiled crown, *ade,* of a type traditionally worn only by those kings who could trace their ancestry to Odudua, the mythic founder and first king of the Yoruba people. The crown is called an *orisha,* a deity, and is the object of ritual attention by a female attendant of the king or, as in the case at the palace in Ila-Orangun, by the senior wife. It is she who places the crown upon the king's head, standing behind the king as she does so; for the king must not look upon the container of powerful medicines, *oogun ashe,* that the herbalist priests have placed in the top of the crown for the protection of the king's head and personal destiny, *ori.* The veil of beads that covers the face of the king not only masks the wearer's individuality, but focuses the viewer's attention upon the real locus of power, the crown, and protects the layman from looking directly upon the face of one whose head and person possess such power. When the king appears wearing the great crown, the chiefs and elders of his town will prostrate themselves before him and proclaim: "The king's power is like unto (or next to) that of the gods," *Oba alaashe ekiji orisha.*

*28½"*                                                                                    *Pace Gallery*

## PLATE 11

These three crowns, of the type known as *orikogbofo,* reveal the impact of Islam and Christianity upon traditional Yoruba forms and ritual iconography. The bronze and gold four-sided conical crown with the beaded tassel hanging at the side suggests the model of the Muslim fez in its form, and the iconoclastic stance of Islam in the absence of traditional iconographic images. There is only the faintest suggestion of the faces of the royal ancestors in the designs on the upper portion. The cylindrical green crown decorated with abstract designs is even further removed from the forms and iconography of traditional crowns, as varied as these were. The gold crown bears the faces of the royal ancestors and has retained the shape of a traditional crown; but the projection from the top is a Christian cross, not the great bird or the gathering of birds or other images suggestive of the powerful medicines, *oogun ashe,* placed within the crown by the herbalist to protect the head of the king. According to the Alake of Abeokuta, a Yoruba king will wear the headdress appropriate to the ceremonies in which he is participating, and will not be governed by his own religious commitments. Hence, at the Muslim celebrations of Ramadan, or the Christian celebrations of Christmas or Easter, the king will appear in a beaded hat which will acknowledge the religious sensibilities of the group, yet affirm the sacredness of his head and his importance as a mediator for all of his people.

A. 8" × 10"  Pace Gallery
B. 6½" × 9½"  Pace Gallery
C. 7¼" × 4¼"  Pace Gallery

## PLATE 12

One of a pair of dance panels, *yata,* worn by a devotee at the annual festival for a Yoruba deity, *orisha.* The blues and golds suggest that the panel was made for a worshipper of *orisha* Oshun, whose priestesses wear silver and lead bracelets on their arms and who carry shining brass bowls to the Oshun River to collect the medicinal waters of the goddess. (Note the depiction of the Oshun worshipper in the *epa* mask, figure 11). The movement from an irregularly checkered horizontal pattern at top and bottom to a vertical pattern in the middle section provides a dynamic background for the singular figure which weaves its way across the surface. Note the suggestion of breasts (or eyes?) near the center of the panel. The distinctive configuration in the midst of repetitive patterns is characteristic of all Yoruba art, as well as of the ritual life.

*11" × 11"*                                                                                     *Pace Gallery*

## PLATE 13

A diviner's bag, *apo Ifa*. The motifs on this extraordinary panel bring together two quite distinctive areas of Yoruba religious life—Ifa divination and the masquerades for the ancestors, *egungun paka*—and suggest that the priest who once used this bag came from a house of patrilineage well known for its powerful ancestral masquerade. The large figure, whose head is blackened from the blood of sacrifices, whose legs are covered with panels of cloths, and whose mid-section radiates power, looks in the direction of a large fleeing black bird. *Egungun* possessing powerful medicine, *oogun,* have power over witches, which are thought to fly as birds in the night, threatening the lives of persons, especially the fertility of women. Bird imagery is prominent in the iconography of Ifa as well; but here the reference is to the ability of the priests to direct the spiritual powers of "our mothers" to positive, creative ends. (See H. Drewal, 1977, p. 11.)

*12" × 12½"*                                                                   *Pace Gallery*

## PLATE 14

Beaded garments, *ewu,* for twin statuettes, *ibeji.* Twins, *ibeji,* are thought to be "spirit children," who can bring to the parents great fortune or misfortune. Thus twin infants receive extraordinary attention, and numerous ritual obligations are performed in relationship to their well-being. Should one of the children die, a diviner will be consulted and, if Ifa advises, a statuette will be carved as a memorial. It will be cared for just as the surviving child, including dressing it with an appropriate garment, *ewu,* in the hope that the dead spirit child will return again in another birth to remain in the home. Although twins are thought to be under the special protection of *orisha* Shango, the greens, golds, browns, and bronzes which are prominent in the *ewu* on the left, colors associated with earth, forest, and medicinal plants, suggest that the owner of this *ibeji* was a priest of Ifa and an herbalist. The blues and golds, as well as the birds on the shoulders and the designs in the upper corners on the *ewu* to the right, suggest an association with *orisha* Oshun and possibly the Palace of Oshogbo.

A. *8" × 11½"*                                          *Pace Gallery*
B. *9" × 10"*                                          *Private Collection*

## PLATE 15

One of a pair of dance panels, *yata,* worn by a devotee at the annual festival for one of the Yoruba deities belonging to a group called "the orisha of the white cloth," *orisha funfun,* among whom are *orisha* Obatala, fashioner of human bodies, *orisha* Osanyin, provider of medicinal herbs, *orisha* Oshun, goddess of life-giving waters, and *orisha* Oko, god of the farm and protector against witches. The tension between energy and structure is visually conveyed by the subtle interplay of light and cool colors among the various geometric patterns. Two faces appear from within and a chameleon rests lightly upon the vibrant surface of the panel. In the Yoruba account of creation the chameleon was the first animal to be placed upon the earth in order to test its firmness in preparation for the arrival of human beings. Like the chameleon, Ifa divination tests the way, reveals the possibilities for one's life and indicates the means for making one's sojourn propitious. Through worship of the *orisha* in praise, prayer, and sacrifice, the life-giving powers that pervade the world can be brought to one's aid.

*11½" × 11½"*                                                                                     *Pace Gallery*

## PLATE 16

A beaded panel, *yata,* worn by priestesses for *orisha* Oshun in the Oshun or Ig-bomina area. At the annual festival for the goddess of medicinal waters, the priestesses, dressed in white wrappers, and with the beaded panels worn hanging down on the left side held by a strap over their shoulders, will carry the shining brass bowls of the deity to the sacred grove at the edge of the Oshun River. There they will make offerings of *akaraoshun,* the bean cakes of Oshun, chant prayers and sing praises to "the owner of all waters/bestower of children," and return to the shrines in their houses with the medicinal waters of the beneficent goddess. As can be seen in this beautiful *yata,* the colors associated with Oshun are gold, silver, and blue. But the touch of the red and white pattern is reminiscent of the fact that according to some Yoruba myths Oshun was once wife to Shango, and on many Oshun shrines an emblem for Shango will be present.

*15″ × 17½″*                                                                 *Private Collection*

## PLATE 17

Three crowns of a type called *orikogbofo,* "head cannot suffer loss," worn on other than ritual occasions. Although the four-sided form, *onigegemerin,* is a recent development in crown making, the cluster of birds on one crown, the faces of the royal ancestors on another, and the projection from the top on all three are characteristic features of old Yoruba crowns. Margaret Drewal has called attention to the fact that projections from the head in Yoruba ritual iconography provide a visual clue to concealed forces that enable the wearer to control and mediate human and supernatural realms; not only in the great crowns (see Plates 10 and 24) worn on ritual occasions, but in the modified projections on a king's everyday headgear, this ancient affirmation of the king's power may be seen (Margaret Drewal, 1977, pp. 43-49). Crown C combines the bird image of traditional Yoruba crowns with a structural design borrowed from the crowns of British monarchs, including clusters of beads imitating diamonds.

A. 7" × 10½"                                    *Pace Gallery*
B. 7½" × 5½"                                    *Pace Gallery*
C. 7½" × 7½"                                    *Private Collection*

## PLATE 18

A diviner's bag, *apo Ifa,* probably from the Oyo area. Colors, as well as geometric patterns and representational images, are an important element in conveying to the Yoruba viewer the hidden power of an object. Yellow and green are associated with Ifa, black and white with Eshu, and red dotted with white is for *orisha* Shango, the deified fourth king of ancient Oyo. Rarely is it one *orisha* who makes claims upon a person. One god may dominate a person's life, shape one's perception of self and world, but others will influence a person's life as well. As the Yoruba dancer must respond to the multiple rhythms of the drums, so the soul attentive to the powers of the *orisha* must somehow respond to their diverse claims.

*13" × 11¾"*                                                           *Private Collection*

## PLATE 19

Beaded sheaths, *ewu orisha Oko,* in which the metal staffs of *orisha* Oko are clothed, *ewu,* when not in ritual use. The red and white vertical stripes on the foreheads of the faces at the top of the sheaths are the marks which a priestess of *orisha* Oko wears on ritual occasions. The animal and bird figures juxtaposed with geometric designs associated with royalty and *orisha,* convey to the informed viewer the nature and extent of the power of the god of the farm, *oko.* In a verbal pun made possible by the tonal language of the Yoruba, the crown, *ade,* rests upon the phallic top, *oko,* of the staff of *orisha* Oko. Thus, the crown-resting-on-phallus refers to the head, *ori,* and power, *ashe,* with which the devotee has identified her own destiny, *ori.*

> *"Orisha Oko, source of wealth.*
> *The one with children owns the world.*
> *The one with children owns the world.*
> *Orisha Oko, Let me give birth to mine."*

> Portion of a song sung by
> Efunwumi, Priestess of *orisha* Oko,
> Ila-Orangun, 1974

A. *51"*
B. *54"*
C. *51"*

*Pace Gallery*
*Private Collection*
*Pace Gallery*

## PLATE 20

Face panel for an *egungun paka* costume. Cowries are a sign of wealth, for they were once the means of economic exchange among the Yoruba. Thus to surround the face of the dancer with cowries is to convey an image of the wealth and power of the lineage for whom the masquerade is danced. The use of beads and the addition of birds suggests the possiblity that the masquerade belonged to a royal house.

*15½" × 14½"*                                                    *Pace Gallery*

## PLATE 21

A panel, *yata*, worn on ritual occasions by a priestess of *orisha* Oshun. Several diviner's bags, *apo Ifa*, in the collection of the Institute of African Studies, University of Ibadan, Nigeria, have a similar beaded fringe. R. F. Thompson refers to a beaded panel with fringe in the UCLA collection as a *yata*, dance panel, worn on festive occasions for the deity Oluwa (see Thompson, 1971, chapter 8, p. 3). The predominant use of gold, blue, and white beads suggests that it is a *yata* panel for the cult of *orisha* Oshun, deity of medicinal waters (see Plate 16).

9¾" × 10½"                                                        *Pace Gallery*

## PLATE 22

A panel worn by a senior priest of Ifa, *babalawo Onifa,* during religous festivals. Its association with Ifa is clearly identified by the gathering of birds, as well as by the division of the composition into four sections, and the prominence of yellow and green in the pattern of colors. On the top of the iron staffs of the priests of Ifa, *opa orere* or *osun,* there is always a large single bird; and on the staffs of the herbalist priest, *opa Osanyin,* there is always a cluster of inward-facing minor birds surmounted by a major bird. Bird imagery suggests the close relationship between the healing arts of divination and herbalism for the Yoruba, and that the healing art depends upon the knowledge of and ability to employ the spiritual force, the generative female power, of "the mothers."

*13½" × 14½"*                                                                 *Pace Gallery*

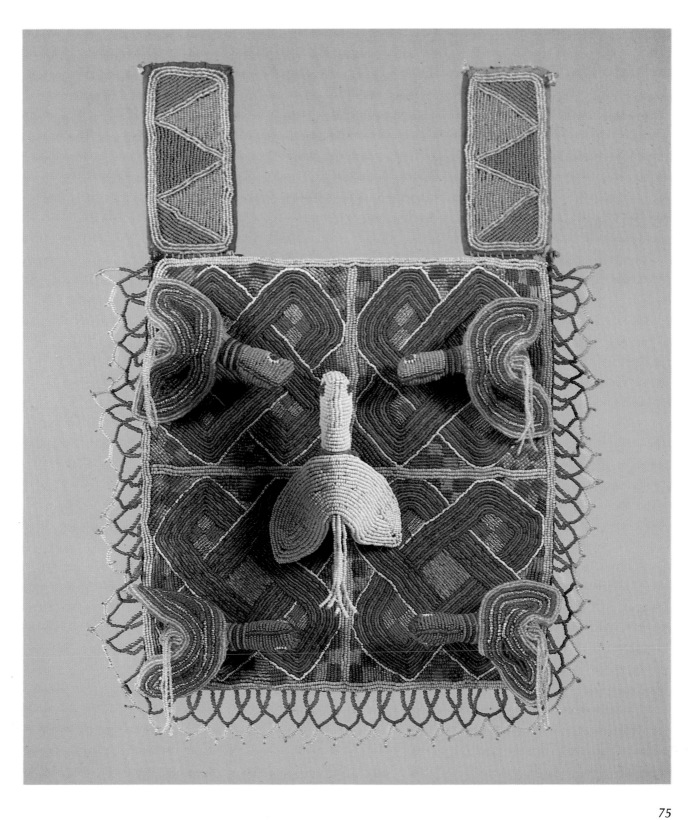

## PLATE 23

A king's crown, *ade,* of the type known as *olojumerindilogun,* "owner of sixteen faces." Accounts vary regarding the reference of the multiple faces on many crowns. Some sources associate them with Odudua, the founder and first king, *oba,* of the Yoruba people, others with Odudua's sixteen sons, who established the legendary sixteen Yoruba kingdoms (note the different descent groups' markings on the faces), and others still with the hierarchic pattern of chieftaincy in Yoruba political life. The theme which links all explanations would appear to be that when a king wears the crown, his head or personal destiny, *ori,* is linked with the awesome power, *ashe,* of the sacred line of Yoruba kings, "a power like that of the gods," *alaashe ekiji orisha.* In the Igbomina town of Ila-Orangun, the chamber in which the great crown is kept, and where on ritual occasions it is placed upon the king's head, is called *ori ojopo,* the chamber "where two destinies meet."

*16"*                                                                 *Private Collection*

## PLATE 24

A king's crown with birds, known as "the great crown," *adenla*. The gathering of birds in a hierarchic pattern, facing the great bird at the crown's peak, expresses the power, *ashe*, of the crown and of the one who wears it. In a literal sense the power is in the crown, for prior to a new crown being worn by a king the leader of the herbalist priests, the *babalawo* Onisegun, must prepare a packet of powerful ingredients, *oogun ashe*, for the protection of the king's head, and place it within the top of the crown, often attaching it to the peg holding the great bird in place. As on the diviner's bag in Plate 22 and on the staffs of the herbalists, the birds surrounding the concealed medicines, and looking upon the great bird "signify that the king himself rules only with the protection and cooperation of the mothers" (H. Drewal, 1977, p. 12). On the front of the crown the birds also surround the head of an elephant, whose great tusks appear also as eyes below which are the incised marks of the royal descent group from Odudua. The projections from the surface of the crown, the vibrant colors and varied background patterns combine to produce an image of immense energy and radiating power.

*41"*                                                               *Ratner Collection*

## PLATE 25

A dance panel, *yata*. The large flattened beads are of a type used before the more common seed beads, indicating that it is especially old, at least early nineteenth century. The panel depicts the figure of Eshu, sometimes referred to as the "trickster" god, but more appropriately understood to be the bearer of sacrifices and the guardian of the ritual process. Similar stick-figure depictions are found on the leather *laba* bags carried by the priest of *orisha* Shango, the god of thunder and lightning, and on the large pots holding the ritual calabash of Eshu on Eshu shrines. In addition, the serrated and tasseled edge of the *laba* Shango is depicted in the pattern at the bottom of this panel. The alternating red and white triangles at the top of the panel form a decorative motif often found on Shango ritual artifacts. The black-edged white rectangle within a red and white border at either side of the panel juxtapose the contrasting colors of Eshu with those of Shango. At the foot of every Shango shrine one finds an emblem, such as cowries embedded in a piece of blackened laterite rock, and a calabash for Eshu.

10¾″ × 11″                                                              *Private Collection*

## PLATE 26

A beaded crown of a type called *orikogbofo,* "head cannot suffer loss," which is worn on other than ritual occasions. The term refers to the need to protect the king's head, *ori,* or personal destiny, from any threat to its power, as, for example, from a curse. The iconography of this crown is similar to the great crowns, *adenla,* (see Plates 10 and 24) but lacks the high conical thrust and the veil of beads. Nonetheless, the crown reminds the one who wears it and the one who sees it that the king's head is sacred, and for the well-being of the town, his power must suffer no diminution. The lettering around the rim of the crown reads: AFAOJA OSHOGBO ATAOJA OSHOGBO, the titles of the king, *oba,* of Oshogbo. The motif of the fish refers to the Oshun cult of the river goddess, whose principle shrine is in Oshogbo.

*11½" × 11"*                                                          *Private Collection*

## PLATE 27

A dance panel, *yata,* probably worn by a priest of Ifa on festival occasions. Henry Drewal observes that the art of the Yoruba "embodies two basic aspects: power concealed within a form and the allusion to this power through visual composition and motifs. While art is visually commanding, it is a hidden presence that determines the attitudes and actions of those who create and use it." (Drewal, 1977, p. 4). The sense of energy, the hidden power of Ifa, is conveyed in the artist's use of bold and subtle geometric forms and colors. The central yellow sphere, filled with tumbling blue, black and white triangles, is surrounded by a series of squares, shimmering with pale blues and reds interspersed with white; and the whole composition is cut diagonally by two strips, dividing the panel into four triangles. This dynamic composition is framed by narrow side panels and a tripartite serrated edge at the bottom with bold red, white, and black patterns. In Yoruba ritual symbolism the number four is associated with Ifa and the number three with the Ogboni cult, worshippers of Onile, the goddess of the earth. In addition, the designs and colors of the borders refer to *orisha* Shango, god of thunder and lightning. Unseen forces of great power are brought together in the visual composition of this *yata.*

*16" × 13"*                                                                                      *Pace Gallery*

## PLATE 28

Beaded sheaths, *ewu,* for the metal staffs, emblems of *orisha* Oko, god of the farm. As in other modes of Yoruba art, the aesthetic of asymmetrical patterns and sharply contrasting colors employed within an encompassing structure suggests the tension, the creative play, between individualism and holism that pervades all of Yoruba life.

A. *47"*                                                              *Pace Gallery*
B. *46"*                                                              *Pace Gallery*
C. *Reverse side of A (detail).*

## PLATE 29

A bead-embroidered garment for deceased twins, *ewu ibeji*. On this rare and beautiful garment the vivid red, white, and gold color scheme and the serrated-edge motif make clear reference to the protective power of *orisha* Shango over these deceased spirit children. On Shango shrines in Oyo, Iwo, and Ila-Orangun one will see *ibeji* statuettes tucked in among the "thunder bolts" in the ritual calabash of Shango or leaning against the pedestal on which the calabash rests. Shango is called "the giver of children, the one who imparts his beauty to the woman with whom he sleeps." But his praise songs attest to the devotee's sense of the dread and uncertainty about Shango's power.

> *Shango kills without warning.*
> *After eating with the elder of the compound*
> *Shango kills his child at the gate.*
> *Shango is a troubled god, like a cloud full of rain.*

Portion of a praise song for Shango
sung by Bamibi Ojo, Ila-Orangun, 1974

10¾ "                                    *Private Collection*

## PLATE 30

A diviner's bag, *apo Ifa.*

In the presence of two Iwori it was said:

> *"The top of the ant-heap resembles a crown.*
> *Leg is used to carry bride-wealth.*
> *The middle is where the cloth is tied.*
> *Camwood's pot dropped to the ground and*
>     *was completely broken.*
> *It was the pot of camwood that dropped*
> *to the ground and was completely broken."*

> *He it was who cast Ifa for ashe (menstrual*
>     *blood), which is woman's power,*
> *He it was who cast Ifa for semen,*
>     *which is heaven's male,*
> *On the day the two of them were coming*
>     *from heaven to earth.*

> *They were told to make sacrifices.*
> *They sacrificed in the creator's house.*
> *They entered the world.*
> *Their talk was as persons.*
> *They became human beings dwelling on earth.*
> *They asked the Iwori to care for them.*
> *It was the Iwori who nursed them,*
>     *when they became human beings.*

> *And those in heaven continue to say:*
>     *"We miss you, for you became children:*
>         *ashe and semen.*
>     *We miss you, for you return no more.*
>     *We miss you, for you became children:*
>         *ashe and semen.*
>     *We miss you, for you return no more.*
>     *We miss you, for you became children."*

A verse from *Odu Iwori Meji,*
recited by *babalawo* Babalola Ifatoogun,
Ibadan, Nigeria, 1972.

*11½" × 13"*                                        Pace Gallery

# BIBLIOGRAPHY

Abimbola, Wande. *Ifa: An Exposition of Ifa Literary Corpus*. Ibadan: Oxford University Press, 1976.

Abraham, Roy C. *A Dictionary of Modern Yoruba*. London: University of London Press, 1958.

Asiwaju, A.I. "Political Motivation and Oral Historical Traditions in Africa: The Case of Yoruba Crowns, 1900-1960." *Africa* 46 (1976): 113-27.

Bascom, William. *African Art in Cultural Perspective: An Introduction*. New York: W.W. Norton & Co., 1973.

———. *Ifa Divination: Communication Between Gods and Men in West Africa*. Bloomington: Indiana University Press, 1969.

———. *The Yoruba of Southwest Nigeria*. New York: Holt, Rinehart and Winston, 1969.

Bascom, William and Paul Gebauer. *Handbook of West African Art*. Milwaukee: Bruce Publishing Co., 1953

Berns, Marla. *Agbaye: Yoruba Art in Context*. Los Angeles: UCLA Museum of Cultural History, 1979.

Bier, H. Ulli. *A Year of Sacred Festivals in One Yoruba Town*, 3rd ed. Lagos: *Nigeria Magazine*, 1959.

———. *The Story of Sacred Wood Carvings from One Small Yoruba Town*. Lagos: *Nigeria Magazine*, 1957.

Carroll, Kevin. *Yoruba Religous Carvings*. New York: Praeger, 1967.

Courlander, H. *Tales of Yoruba Gods and Heroes*. New York: Crown, 1973.

Daniel, F. "Beadworkers of Illorin, Nigeria." *Man* 37 (2): 7-8.

Davidson, Basil. *Africa: History of a Continent*. London: Hamlyn, 1972.

Drewal, Henry J. *African Artistry: Technique and Aesthetics in Yoruba Sculpture*. Atlanta: The High Museum, 1980.

———. *Traditional Art of the Nigerian Peoples: The Milton D. Ratner Family Collection*. Washington, D.C.: Museum of African Art, 1977.

Drewal, Margaret Thompson. "Projections from the Top in Yoruba Art." *African Arts* 11 (October 1977): 43-49.

Eluyemi, O. "Treasures in Yoruba Palaces." *Gangan* (Ibadan) 7 (January 1977): 8-14.

Fagg, William. *African Tribal Images*. Cleveland: Cleveland Museum of Art, 1968.

———. *The Living Arts of Nigeria*. London: Studio Vista, 1970.

———. *Nigerian Images*. New York: Praeger, 1963.

Fagg, William and Frank Willett. "Ancient Ife: An Ethnological Survey." *Odu* 8 (1960): 21-35.

Fagg, William and Margaret Plass. *African Sculpture: An Anthology*. London: Dutton Vista, 1966.

Northern, Tamara. *The Sign of the Leopard: Beaded Art of Cameroon*. Storrs: The William Benton Museum of Art, the University of Connecticut, 1975.

Ogunba, O. "Crowns and 'Okute' at Idowa." *Nigeria* 83 (December 1964): 249-62.

Pemberton, John. "A Cluster of Sacred Symbols: Orisha Worship Among the Igbomina Yoruba of Ila-Orangun." *History of Religions* 7 (August 1977): 1-28.

———. "Egungun Masquerades of the Igbomina Yoruba," *African Arts* 11 (April 1978): 40-47.

———. "Eshu-Elegba: the Yoruba Trickster God." *African Arts* 9 (October 1975): 20-27, 66-70.

―――. "Sacred Kingship and the Violent God: the Worship of Ogun Among the Yoruba." *Berkshire Review,* Special Issue on Culture and Violence (Fall 1979): 85-106.

Pokornowski, Ila. "Beads and Personal Adornment." *Fabrics of Culture: The Anthropology of Clothing and Adornment,* edited by Justine M. Cordwell and Ronald A. Schwarz. New York: Mouton, 1979.

Rubin, Arnold. *Yoruba Sculpture in Los Angeles Collections.* Claremont: Montgomery Art Center, Pomona College, 1969.

Siroto, Leon. *African Spirit Images and Identities.* New York: Pace Editions Inc., 1976.

―――. "Twins of Yorubaland." *Bulletin of the Field Museum of Natural History* 38 (July 1967): 4-8.

Stoll, Mareidi and Gert, and Ulrich Klever. *Ibeji: Twin Figures of the Yoruba.* Munich: 1980.

Thompson, Robert F. *African Art in Motion: Icon and Act.* Los Angeles: University of California Press, 1974.

―――. *Black Gods and Kings: Yoruba Art at UCLA.* Los Angeles: University of California Press, 1971.

―――. "The Sign of the Divine King: An Essay on Yoruba Bead-Embroidered Crowns with Veil and Bird Decoration." *African Arts* 3 (Spring 1970).

Willett, Frank. *African Art: An Introduction.* New York: Praeger, 1971.

*Fig. 16: Top view of
informal crown.
See Plate 28C.*

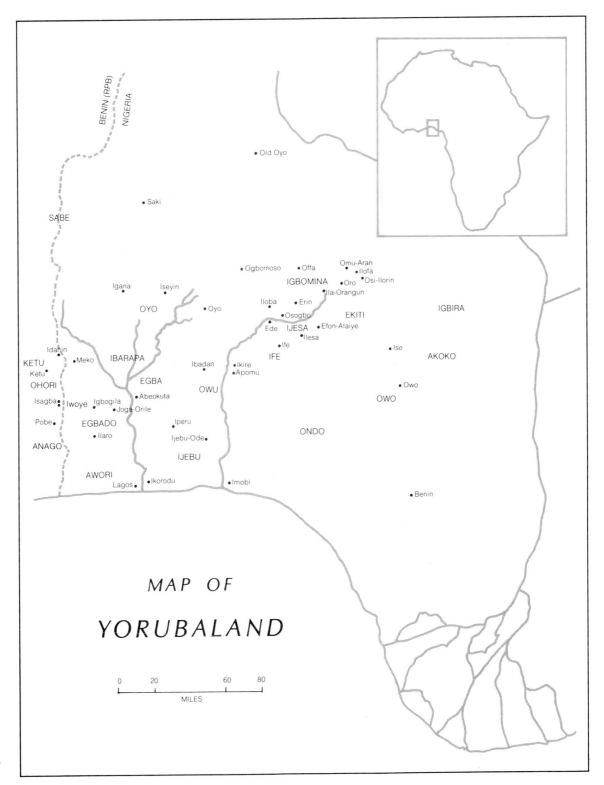

# MAP OF
# YORUBALAND

*Map by
Henry Drewal,
1980.*

# CREDITS

*Fig. 18: Detail of Plate 30.*